Laptop Millionaire I

How to Create a Million Dollar Business While Living as a Carefree Soul-Led Gypsy Wanderer!

International Amazon Best-Selling Author Katrina Ruth
(formerly Kat Loterzo)

Published by: Katrina Ruth
Edited by: Deanna Shanti – Shanti Publishing
Copyright © 2019 Katrina Ruth

www.thekatrinaruthshow.com

ISBN: 978-0-9945847-9-3

Receive your FREE Video Training on 'Choosing Faith Over Fear to Create the Business and Life You're Meant For' By choosing Faith over Fear I've now created a multi 7-figure purpose led empire, from soul. A **HELL YES** life!

Let's talk about how to do just that for you here:

https://thekatrinaruthshow.com/faithvsfearfreetraining

For more kickass books for kickass women, including free downloads:

www.booksforkickasswomen.com

Contents

INTRODUCTION

Do you remember back when you were 20, or perhaps 23, and 30 seemed like the oldest possible age in the WORLD?

I remember being so damn certain that by 30 I'd have it ALL going on, and then some!

I was going to be a millionaire ... of course!

Have a GREAT Vogue-esque house in a great area.

Be happily married with the requisite 2.4 kids.

Be an author, a speaker, a raving success!

It was going to be incredible, I knew it! And I had so much time as well, I mean GOD ... 30!

Wanna know something really cool? I got on the right track well in advance!

By 25 years old I was married, living in a great inner Melbourne trendy apartment, had a BMW and a $20,000 surround system, was being paid well in a great managerial role and on the fast-track to climbing the ladder ALL the way high! Perks and travel trips and the right clothes and a great social set rounded it out. Boo-yah! Nobody could touch me and I was going to MAKE it!

What a smart girl!

Of course there was just ONE tiny hiccup that kinda threw me off path shortly after that period ... isn't there always a hiccup of some kind; just when you think you've got it all figured out??!

In my case the hiccup was kind of, well, kind of a big deal. Isn't it always ... really? I mean when you look back isn't there ALWAYS something major that threw you totally OFF course but that if you really think about threw you quite nicely ON track in the end?

In the end ...

But before the end, for me, came this:

By 27 years old, I was done.

Divorced.
Broken.
Insomniac.
Bulimic.
Mess.

Oh, and I'd quit the job, walked away from the apartment and car and all the perks and even lost all my life savings.

So much for fucking rocking it by 30!

Walking out of my marriage was one of the hardest things I've ever done, but I'll be honest with you:

I did it like I was on auto-pilot.

I did it in a very messy, very public, very sabotag-y kind of a way.

I saw exactly what I was doing, and I just ... let it happen. It was like I almost couldn't control myself, like as he at one point begged me to stay and I just refused but inside of me I was screaming stay! stay! stay! NOBODY ELSE WILL EVER LOVE YOU!

But I couldn't make myself say the words even though I was SURE it was an insanely stupid thing to do.

So much for the plan, hey?!

And just to top it all off I had NO fucking clue what I really wanted to do with my life, or who I even was. I felt ... washed up. Lost. Not HOPELESS as I still always believed in the big things, but I guess for the first time in my life I was really having to face up to the reality that if it was going to happen?

I was going to have to make it happen!

And guess what.. I DID #obviously!

Have you ever had a wake-up call in your life, where you just realise -

Oh fuck. If I want what I say I want and have always thought I am DEFINITELY going to get then I'm going to have to actually CHANGE things? And maybe I don't feel ready to change things, or know how, or even where to start?

That's how I felt.

In Laptop Millionaire Badass I take you through just how I brought all my dreams to life! So you too can press the fuck play on yours and begin creating your million dollar business while living as a carefree soul-led gypsy wanderer!

Let me ask you a question, when you look back 10 years from now, do you think you'd regret more that you stayed, settled, played it safe or that you gave your true dreams a red hot go?

This is your life gorgeous.

You only get to live it once.

Are you okay with getting old like this or are you ready to do whatever it takes, for as long as it takes to become the Laptop Millionaire BADASS you know you are!? It IS possible, I did it and so too can you!

Dreams only come true if you chase them gorgeous, so let's get to and chase them together, right NOW!

CHAPTER 1 - I DID IT!

It was way back in 2011 when I first realised that I'd done it. I remember turning to my partner at the time and saying, "do you realise that with where my business is at now, we could actually just travel anytime ... or even permanently?!"

Pretty cool feeling.

And not without reason, either, because when I began blogging in 2007 one of the first things I said to myself was that I was going to become location independent.

I remember even first HEARING about the idea of being able to work from anywhere ... do what you want ... just sit and write from cafes by the beach, and have that be your biz; your LIFE!

Want to know where I am right now as I write this?

Sitting in beautiful Bali at my hotel restaurant just metres from the waves.

Want to know where I am when I'm at my 'base' on Australia's beautiful Gold Coast?

About fifty metres from the beach, when I walk out the door of my building.

I created my dream in my mind. And then I lived into it. I continue to!

Actually, where I am at ANY given time is I'm wherever I WANT to be, and this is what dreaming like this is all about.

My dream was to travel the world permanently with my family for several years, and from June 2014 we did exactly that. Dozens of countries ... endless adventures ... and my biz and income GREW during that time. I had my first 100k month while lofting it out in Soho New York.

And here's the thing ... your biz ALWAYS grows when you follow alignment!

I LOVE being location free.

Sometimes that means staying right there at 'home' in Australia.

Other times it means six + different countries in a month.

Or perhaps it means packing up your 4-week-old baby and hitting the road as we did!

Or maybe just waking up one morning and deciding to get out of dodge.

There are no rules. With kids, without kids, with a million dollar+ biz already, or not.

In fact, when I first left, my finances were still a mess!! Saying yes to my DREAM gave me motivation to up my game.

Don't you notice that always happens?

I've done it all.

And I continue to follow my heart!

Are you following yours?

CHAPTER 2 -AND THEN I JUST DECIDED TO WRITE

For as long as I can remember I always knew I wanted to be a writer.

I was on this pathway of being the GOOD student and girl, I was top of every class academically, always, and the PLAN was to become a lawyer.

Got the grades for it, too, started studying Arts and was going to switch into Law/Arts, but within less than a week at University it hit me:

I'm not going to do this, actually.

Nobody is watching to make sure I show up.

Nobody even knows!

I look back now, and it's clear that a big part of why I pushed myself so much to ALWAYS be the best, at school, was because I wanted the validation of being TOLD I was the best.

At Uni I didn't get that instant feedback, and to top it off I guess I just realised, Huh. I don't think I WANT to do this whole normal life thing, actually.

Growing up it wasn't ALWAYS about becoming a lawyer. That basically became a pathway because a) I liked to argue and win (haha, what a shock), and b) it was a good EGO goal to chase.

If I'm a lawyer then I must be SUCCESSFUL!

The other thing, though, which I remember thinking about doing a LOT, was being a writer. By writer I meant 'journalist', since in school that's the logical career outcome version of wanting to write.

I mean, really - you don't get a career as a writer like an AUTHOR or something, do you? That's not very practical! And what other ways are there to write anyway?

So, simple:

Become a lawyer or become a journalist.

Going back further than that and as far as what I can remember, since I was very, very small, it was artist.

Funny...

How we always end up back where it was we started, where our dreams began, where WE began.

If you think about it, you've ALWAYS known what it is you're meant to be doing!

Haven't you?

Of course, when we're young and we have these dreams, these desires, this calling, and this thing that says -

"I just want to create"

We don't know HOW on earth to DO that.

How do I be an artist, what does that even mean? Okay, I don't know how, so maybe I want to be a writer, but how do I do THAT?!

Be a journalist, hmmm ... okay be a lawyer! That's a fancy job! Career counsellor approved, and everything!

Let's do it.

And then ...

Well, then.

You embark, don't you, upon the normal life. Trying so DESPERATELY hard to actually get it to work!

And it just -

Doesn't.

Quite.

Seem to FEEL like it should.

I don't know about you, but I've just never been that GOOD at following through on things that don't FEEL good, y'know?

And I might tell myself ALL the stories in the world about how I'm GOING TO DO IT THIS TIME, NO REALLY FOR REAL!

I've done it with study.

I've done it with jobs.

I've done it with RELATIONSHIPS.

I've even done it with diets and training regimes!

And in the end, but ONLY 100% of the time, if it's not a FIT for me and I mean a SOUL fit, I find myself -

Walking away.

And when I say walking? I mean RUNNING LIKE A BAT OUT OF HELL, #stealthexit style, normally.

Now you see her -

Now you don't!

lol.

I always did love that movie ... I always did love ANYTHING that was about DISAPPEARING, escaping, whoosh -

buh bye.

Still do ;)

And what it was, REALLY, was that deep inside of me I did just KNOW -

(As I know you do too)

- I wasn't born for this whole ... LIFE thing. NOT LIKE THIS. I'm going to do it MY way ... somehow! Even though I don't really know what that is or how it would look or ANY of it.

But I'll figure it the fuck OUT, just TRY TO STOP ME!

Of course, here is the truth. The truth which it took me some time to admit to myself, and perhaps you too. PERHAPS YOU'RE LYING TO YOURSELF THIS VERY SECOND ABOUT IT!

And the truth is this:

The ONLY thing, the only PERSON, who ever tried to STOP me, was me.

Because other people, with their well-or-not-intentioned suggestions or even COMMANDS, do not actually get to choose how you play life. The GREAT news is that YOU get to do that.

The sobering news, perhaps, is that YOU GET TO DO THAT AND ALSO YOU MUST.

It's actually not optional, y'know ...

EITHER way you're choosing! So, if you look around right now and you don't LOVE WHAT YOU SEE, or if you look inside right now and if you don't ADORE how you feel, or if you look to the future right now and you're not just so GEE-

DARN excited and gleeful and grateful about it, then get a fucking grip baby.

You did this.

You did ALL of it.

The ball was squarely in your court since the day you were FORMED, in fact, because God gave us the gift of INFINITE choice.

It's a blessing.

It's a responsibility.

It's EXCITING!

And it's just motherfucking FACT.

And here is what else:

This idea that you have, which perhaps you've not really stopped and thought about or else you'd realise how non-sensical it is, that there should be somebody TELLING YOU HOW TO PLAY LIFE - your life! - telling you how to travel your own pathway, well -

That idea is gonna have to go.

You're not a child anymore.

Dreaming of being an artist.

Knowing that someday, someway you will be.

And you're also not a teenager being told by the world - and LISTENING - that there is a right or a wrong way to do life 'properly'.

Are you??!

So why are you acting it?

You're an adult now, and if you want it to happen you damn sure KNOW you can make it happen but you also gotta go DO that.

Whatever it takes.

No matter what it takes.

Until it takes.

Yes?

YES.

And you get to choose to keep the childlike wonder and the dreaming and the playfulness, or you get to choose to bring it in NOW, that's the beautiful thing! Life just gets better and better the further along you go.

I think that one of the most powerful lessons we can each learn about life is not how to go out there, learn to succeed or achieve, find or build a roadmap to wealth, acclaim, respect, worthiness!

It's that the answers were already there.

The entire freaking time.

I know for me, I spent so many years wandering and looking and trying to try, all of the things I was told I should.

And then?

I just decided to write.

CHAPTER 3 - HOW COMMITTED ARE YOU TO CREATING YOUR DREAM LIFE?

In 2007, when I was 26, I created my first blog at www.playlife.com.au. I had no idea what I was doing with it or where I was going to go with it; in fact the reason I got started writing online was in order to add value to my personal training business.

But I also wasn't naive enough to not know that there was a world of possibility opening up with blogging and online marketing, and even though it was a world I knew little about, I knew this - somehow, some way, I was going to become part of it. Big time.

I'd always dreamed of being a writer, and I'd always known I'd be an entrepreneur, and this seemed the perfect mix. I'd read stories of other Aussie bloggers making as much as $80k per year, working a few hours a day from a cafe. It absolutely sounded too good to be true and I absolutely knew that if other people really were doing it?

Then there was no reason on earth I shouldn't also.

And even though I can't remember most of what I actually did back then in my quest to make a name for myself, I remember one thing very, very clearly. In the very early days, I made the following blood-oath promise to myself-

No matter what, I will never ever, ever quit. No matter what, I will just keep going until I get there.

'There' hadn't even been fully defined (and in fact wasn't for at least my first three or four years online!) but I knew generally what I meant.

Okay it wasn't 'actually' a blood oath promise. But seriously? I would say it's among the top two or three most strongly felt commitments I've ever made to myself. Right now, the only one I can think of that would equal it in its strength is the promise I made to myself to get back in shape after having a baby.

In both cases, there was no maybe. Which meant also - there was no chance of anything less than total success.

How Committed Are You to Creating Your Dream Life?

When you want something badly enough - and you also firmly believe it is possible - nothing and nobody can get in your way.

Of course, for most people, the thing that does get in their way and stop them from making their dreams reality is, quite simply and sadly, themselves.

The truth is that it's just not good enough to set yourself a goal or dream shrouded in words like 'I hope' and 'I'll try', even 'I'll do my very best'.

Despite my determination in the tale above, I've been guilty of this wishy-washy approach to creating my dream business and life over and over again.

The most relevant example, as I write this, is about the very topic of dream life creation. For years I've known that what I really want to be known for is for being a transformative speaker and author who empowers other women to create their best life. Yet while I've certainly woven in a lot of talk and work on mindset and creating your reality, what I really built my brand on is fat loss and nutrition with a dash of inner work thrown in.

Why not really do exactly what I wanted to do until now?

Well - I did. I tried. I produced an online bootcamp on creating your dream life. I put together some coaching offers along those lines, even a workshop. It all did okay. But not as good as my fat loss products and programs. But hey, at least I tried, right?

NO.

When success is the only option - the ONLY option and you will not take anything less - there is no try.

Have you ever made up your mind that you will have something, that you WILL make it reality, that it IS happening no matter what? Have you ever felt this way and then also fully believed it to be possible?

If you have you know that nothing - NOTHING - can stop you until you get there.

But in the same vein, you know that the things you try your hand at - even give your very best shot - they just don't work quite so well, do they?

Think back. What are some of the things you've tried really hard to create in your life?

Perhaps you've had a crack at making money online. Spent money, time, energy on it. Given it a LOT of effort and attention.

Perhaps like me, you've tried to go from 'just' making money online to making money online doing what you love.

Perhaps you've tried to get back in shape, or in shape in the first place.

To overcome a poor relationship with food and your body.

To find love.

To improve your current relationship.

To keep a tidy home.

To save up for your dream _____.

To take a certain number of weeks off each year.

Me, I've tried all sorts of things! -

Getting 'full abs' for a fitness model style photo shoot.

Being published in various major media publications.

Becoming known as an author and speaker (outside of my own circle).

Taking the whole weekend off :)

Sprinting up the 1000 stairs again without a rest (used to do that all the time, been trying to do it again since about 2002).

Winning a novice bodybuilding competition.

Paying off credit card debt in a given period of time.

Saving a certain amount of money in a given period of time.

The common thread in all of these things is not that I didn't want them as badly as I wanted my online success, or to get my pre-baby body back, or to have more fun and closeness in my marriage.

The common thread is, quite simply, that I didn't make any of the above things a true 'must'.

A mixture of fear, and 'what if' and not fully believing I could and not being willing to pay the price.

But what it really comes down to - and I'm speaking for you as well as me here - is that we simply weren't fully committed to making these dreams reality.

Justify all you like but here's an unignorable FACT about life and how you get to live it -

Whatever you fully commit yourself to and also choose to believe possible, will be yours.

Ah ah - no buts.

Anything you fully commit to, and also choose to believe possible, WILL be yours.
Don't believe me? That's your choice, but it's to your detriment. So why not make a new choice?

Because here's the thing.

Right now, I know you have goals.

I know you have dreams, ideas, and visions of how your life will be one day, when it's ideal.

Let's pick just one, for now. Go on - choose your dream. What is it?

My dream is to _____.

Okay. Now perhaps this dream or goal is clearly mapped out in your mind, on a vision board, in your journal, or perhaps it's a little hazy around the edges.

But, when it comes to your success, there is really only one thing that matters right now and that's this -

Are you FULLY committed to making this dream a reality?

Will you do whatever it takes and keep going for however long it takes until you get there?

Do you BELIEVE it can happen for you?

Are you prepared to pick yourself up 1000 times over and then 1000 more and then again and again until you get there, if you don't succeed at first?

When you think about this goal, what language do you use?

I hope ...

I'll try ...

If .... then I'll be able to ...

I just have to ... then I can ...

One day ...

Or do you use language like this -

I will.

I AM.

This is happening.

No matter what.

I have no idea how but I'll figure it out.

And even - in advance -

I HAVE.

And thank you.

Do you grit your teeth and keep moving forward even when people are mocking you, rolling their eyes, wondering when you're going to grow up?

Do you push through when it's exhausting, when you feel as though you're completely wasting your time and as though nothing is changing?

Do you try again and again and again and again and NEVER accept that you've reached the end until you have, in fact, reached your goal?

Do you go to bed at night thinking about it, wake up in the morning ready to work on it, prioritise it above the busy work and shoulds of your never-ending task list?

Do you surround yourself with people, affirmations, beliefs, books that will move you toward your goal?

Do you look for case studies of people just like you or perhaps 'worse off' than you who've achieved such a goal, and use them to inspire yourself?

Do you claim your success every damn day, days, weeks, months or even years before it has happened?

Do you keep your eye on the prize and refuse to be swayed by the naysayers, particularly that sneaky negative part of your own mind?

Do you train your mind, your body, your beliefs, your actions, like a warrior? Do you push yourself to become stronger, faster, more powerful, more unstoppable, like a force against nature, always ready for battle, always willing to fight, never ready to fall no matter how bloodied and brutal it gets out there?

Or are you more 'realistic' than that?

The road to my online success and now being able to make money doing what I love and living a GREAT lifestyle has not been a quick one, nor an easy one. There are many who have done it faster and better than me.

But there are even more - untold millions, really - who fell by the wayside long ago and whose dreams are long forgotten; even by them.

They are the ones who were realistic.

Who tried.

Who 'did everything'.

Who gave it their best shot.

Who finally fell for the last time and did not get up again.

Right now, you have an incredible and immeasurable power in your hands. Right now, you have the ability to decide who you will be, what you will have, what you will experience in your life.

You can choose anything you like, anything at all.

But just for starters, how about you choose this one very simple thing -

To keep going until you get there.

CHAPTER 4 - YOUR MILLION DOLLAR BUSINESS IS YOU

For the longest time I struggled to find the one true path that would help me to really grow my brand, position myself as THE expert in my field, help me reach the millions of people I know I'm born to reach, and of course also make the millions of dollars that so many of us dream about.

Have you ever spent AGES pushing for something only to find it was right there the whole time?

The truth is, I spent a helluva lot of money learning a helluva lot of stuff. To be precise, somewhere in the neighbourhood of $300,000. This was, largely, either every cent I earned throughout that same period of time or simply whacked on the credit card. Enter: $100k+ debt and a business that, five or six or perhaps eight years later, I'm no longer really sure when I should count BACK to, still wasn't working.

And the thing is -

I knew my shit.

I mean I KNEW my shit.

I could talk optins and lead gen and conversions and funnels with the best of 'em. Okay maybe not the BEST of them (testing and measuring remains my bug bear to this day; I much prefer to just merrily create and be on my way!) but I definitely KNEW some shit.

What's more, it was GOOD shit. And certainly, LEARNED from the best.

Did I implement it?

You bet your ass I did! I'm an A CLASS student! I ALWAYS implement.
And therein lies the rub ...

(And perhaps you can relate)

When I got into this game, it was because I kinda couldn't help myself. I had things to SAY God darn it! A MESSAGE to share! Stuff I needed to TELL THE WORLD! I wanted to be a writer! A speaker! An entrepreneur! A THOUGHT LEADER and a game changer, no less!

I was going to change the world, I just knew it! And I started to, in my own small way, but soon enough I realised -

There's so much I don't know.

There's even more that I don't even know I don't know!

One of my earlier mentors called my sales processes CUTE for heavens sakes! I had to lift my game. I had to learn the STRATEGIES of online sales and marketing, and then, clearly, if I was actually going to 'make it' as a business coach I was going to have to TEACH those strategies.

Never mind that moving away from my heart stuff and into the pure head work of TOTAL strategy and strategy alone wasn't working for ME, I'd teach it to others and I'd be GOOD at it.

After all -

That's what my clients wanted.

It's what the industry wanted.

It's where the MONEY was, amiright?

Only thing is.
And it's kind of a LITTLE thing.

(But still maybe worth saying)

It didn't fucking work!

I had strategies coming out of my strategies! I planned, and I drafted, and I funnelled my little heart out and it didn't. fucking. work. Not for me, not really. And not for my clients, not really.

Have you ever realised you've been focusing on everything BUT the one thing you really need to focus on?

Oh SURE. There was some money.

A little. Then some more. Then not much. Then less still.

And some response.

A little. Then some more. Then not much. Then less still.

It cycled back and forth enough that it was easy to tell myself -

This is how it is.

And to tell my clients -

That's the way this works.

You gotta push! You gotta hustle! You gotta work HARD for the money! Do more! Be more! Do it all! Do it now!

Yes.

But also.

No.

Not UNLESS.

You have the ONE THING IN PLACE FIRST.

You know about the one thing, right?

The one thing is the ONE THING, that by doing, or implementing, or being it, you make everything else EASIER or even not NECESSARY.

The one thing should, of course, relate to your biggest dream and goal.

(You do know your biggest dream and goal, right?)

In my business, my greatest dream and goal is to impact the lives of millions of people to get their butts into alignment and press play NOW as the leader and game-changer they are born to be. A side-effect of achieving this goal, which I'm quite okay with, is that I make multiples of millions. And some other stuff, but that's the crux of it.

And it turned out, that I truly DID have some shit-hot strategies in place and I truly DID know what I was on about, but I didn't have the ONE THING going on.

The INFURIATING part of it was that I so desperately WANTED to have the one thing going on, but I'd created a way of acting within my business that caused me to believe I couldn't AFFORD to have the one thing going on. Yet. When all the while I couldn't afford NOT to!

And so, I fought and I pushed and I worked and I followed the damn RULES and it did WORK ... sort of.
But it didn't WORK. You know?

When I introduced the one thing, something magical happened.

And it truly happened overnight, in the blink of an eye, like nothing I've ever seen before. All of a sudden, everything just FLOWED ...

All of a sudden, MONEY flowed ...

All of a sudden, people started KNOWING me ...

TALKING about me ...

Wanting to WORK with me ...

It was an INFLUX, a RUSH, a TIDAL WAVE.

And I realised -

For fuck's sakes. I really could have had this all along! If only I'd known. Which really meant - if only I'd listened.

Do you ever feel that way?

Have you ever?

Do you, now?

You know what the one thing is, right?

It's me, being me.

And it's you, being you.

That's it baby. Your million-dollar business is not the right strategy.

It's not the next program.

It's not a more carefully engineered launch.

It's nothing, nothing at all that you can find outside yourself.

The million-dollar business is you baby. Time to let the world have some of that good stuff.

CHAPTER 5 - ALL I DO TO MAKE MY MILLIONS IS LIVE MY GOD DAMN AWESOME LIFE, AND SHOW IT TO THE INTERNET

The thing you have to understand, if you truly want to make millions by 'being you', is that you need to STOP doing all the shit that is not in fact 'you being you', when it comes to working on or in your biz.

You know - the stuff you hate, or just don't like, or it drains you, or it's freaking tedious? The stuff you do when you're not doing what you REALLY want to do and what feels in flow for you?

YES. THAT'S THE STUFF I'M TELLING YOU TO QUIT!! THE BAD YUCKY ANNOYING STUFF!

I know, right? Quelle idee! Isn't business supposed to be about pushing shit up a HILL? Doing stuff you don't really love (or flat out despise)? Doing it in a way that goes against your natural style? Doing it in a way that exhausts your energy and drains your SOUL? Doing it and also having to, as part of it, deal with people you don't REALLLLLLY like that much (aka find annoying as fuck and why won't they go AWAY?!).

Well -

No, actually.

I don't believe that business - the business of being YOU and also the business of BRANDING you and your true message - should be about doing stuff that cannot be counted as YOU BEING YOU, the best of you!

I know we grow up believing that 'work' means going against our nature, or at the very least it's something you do when you're not having fun or just living your LIFE, but I thought the whole point of building a personal brand in which you share what's inside of you is that it's supposed to be about just living your life.

And letting people in.

Right?

And I know it seems like a pipe dream to imagine that every day you could get to wake up and just be you, the you who you want to be, follow the flow and do | create
| unleash what excites and moves you, and that you could get paid for that; even help others - a LOT of 'em - to get more out of THEIR lives, but it's REALLY, REALLY NOT.

You can wake up every day.

Follow your heart.

Be and do and create from what's inside of you and what just FEELS right and true.

And make MILLIONS OF FUCKING DOLLARS FOR THAT.

But guess what?

Not only are you going to have to accept that as POSSIBLE (possible for YOU baby, not just possible in general!), but - and this is the bit most people will categorically FAIL at - it's definitely taken me up until VERY recently to fully get - you'll also have to DUMP the stuff that does not feed into you following your heart.

And your logical mind, the part of you that refuses to believe it could be that good or that easy is gonna FIGHT THIS LIKE A BANSHEE.

That doesn't make it any less true though!

Think about it -

If the way to get paid for being you is to BE you, then any time you're NOT DOING THAT you're costing yourself.

You think that there's ALL THIS OTHER STUFF that has to be done, in order to build your following, create, market, and sell stuff, deliver it, deal with the behind the scenes of it all, etc, but ACTUALLY all of that is more than taken care of when you simply act from what's within, and let people see it.

Want to grow your email list? Document some part of your life that's of value and let people have it in exchange for their email address. Keep the tech and 'putting together' / fancifying how it looks side of things AS MINIMAL AS FUCKING POSSIBLE.

It doesn't MATTER how it all looks, not really. POLISHED and PRETTY and PERFECT doesn't make you millions, and it sure as shit doesn't allow you to be FULFILLED.

Content does.

Creating it.

From the heart.

Just by waking up and doing YOU.

So, you can take your pretty website or whatever else ideas and shove 'em up your ass if you think that worrying about all that shit is a valid cause to delay on BEING YOU AND LETTING PEOPLE SEE IT for even another moment.
Get it out there.

Get it done.

Correct later.

I've only JUST started worrying about shit like that, and I'm ten years and millions of bucks in!! And when I say worrying about it I mean I now get to pay other people to worry about it, but we STILL keep the putting together of shit VERY freaking basic.

Oh, and I can afford to pay other people to worry about it because, you know, I spent my time over the years just BEING ME and writing and speaking about it. Documenting it.

What else?

Want to have a more powerful brand? Create more content. Document what YOU do. Share how you do it. Share the mindset and the thought processes, and how you got there. Share live examples, or breakdowns thereof, where you can.

Want to MARKET more effectively? Create more content. Document YOUR success. Show the behind the scenes. PUBLISH IT EVERYWHERE.

Want to SELL more effectively? Create.more.content. Get people excited and inspired by showing them what's possible. Let 'em see all of it, don't hold anything back! Then? Simply ask (and tell; nothing wrong with TELLING!) them to buy.

Oh, and for what they should buy?

Really? I mean, you really gotta ask that?!

CONTENT BABY.

DOCUMENT YOUR LIFE.

THE REALLY JUICY BITS.

THE DETAIL OF HOW YOU GOT THERE AND HOW YOU CONTINUE TO.

SHOW THEM HOW YOU DO YOU AND TELL THEM HOW IT IS YOU THINK THAT ALLOWS YOU TO DO YOU SO DAMN WELL.

Give them exercises based on what YOU do.

Give them actions based on what YOU do.

Show them how to overcome or elevate their inner shit based on what YOU do!

The ONLY reason you could possibly feel like you need to argue against any of this is if you DON'T THINK YOUR LIFE IS WORTH OBSERVING!!

Which is to say -

You don't think you have a message.

Or something powerful inside.

Or that you've achieved anything.

In which case -

GO AND FIGURE THAT SHIT OUT.

But I THINK you KNOW you've got that stuff. I think you could stand to give yourself just a little bit more CREDIT about how powerful you are when you just wake up and be you each day. I think that if you let people see the way you think | show up | create | achieve | BE that they could learn a helluva lot -

Just by observing.

And if you were to in some way PACKAGE that shit and show people the inside your head side of it, as well as break it down for them?

Well.

You might just build a multi-million-dollar empire, simply by waking up every day, doing what you love, and being you.

Seems to be what I did, somehow!

Look -

I know it's normal and natural and easy to think that it can't BE so simple. That if you're not fighting against yourself and pouring your time, your soul, your life into shit that LESSENS you, then you're not doing it right.

But the REALITY is just not so.

I know for a FACT that the more I ignore ALL THE OTHER STUFF and just do what I wanna do, go completely from my heart and from flow, and then simply write | speak | create

I sell about it, the more money I make and also the more of a purposeful IMPACT I'm able to create.

And without fail, every single time I tell myself I 'have to' sit down and suck it up and do shit that drains or just bores me, or that I find painstaking or flat out painFUL, it not only is time lost from creating and documenting what would actually HELP you, but there is also a carry on effect of BLAH which absolutely impacts what else I create and unleash that day, that week, etc.

I implore you to think about this:

If right now you're spending even 50% of your time doing shit that does not comprise YOU BEING YOU and letting people see it - and I'll bet most people reading this are spending 90% of their time on it actually - then WHAT IMPACT IS THAT HAVING ON YOU BEING ABLE TO ACTUALLY BRAND YOU?

In the end, you can sit back and say you learned everything you needed to know about internet marketing, and your landing pages looked great, ETC. -

Or you can sit here with me and say that all you actually do each day?

Is live your God damn awesome life and show it to the internet.

CHAPTER 6 - FALL IN LOVE WITH SOMETHING, AND DO IT FOR LIFE

What it's all supposed to be about really, this whole quest we're on, indeed - I believe! - your whole raison d'etre, is to find the thing you are not only wildly passionately deeply crazy in love with NOW but know you will be for life.

The thing you will live for, breathe for, give your all for, until you ultimately die for it.

If you've been lucky enough to find that thing already, if right now you KNOW as you read this what it is, you already feel the rise of your heart beating just from thinking about it, being reminded of it, KNOWING it, I hope you know how damn fortunate you are. I commend you for being conscious enough to have RECOGNISED it when it first came to you.

So many don't.

So many won't.

So many think that the dreams and the excitement and the feel of THRILL we get when we know are relics of childhood or the years before we Became Responsible Adults, and that it's irresponsible to act on those feelings or even to give them any mind. There's too much to be done, after all!

Well, personally I'd rather be an irresponsible adult for life as far as the rules of normal society go, if it means I can follow my heart, follow the THRILL.

Wouldn't you?

The thing is ... I KNOW you would. I know you hear me, you feel me, you ARE me and I am you and our hearts beat in unison to the tune of CREATION and FREEDOM and doing what others WON'T in order to live as they CAN'T, and going where the wild things are which is to say going OH - !

So deep within our own hearts, our own souls, our very cells, in order to let out -

What always had to come out.

I know that you, as me, understand that the entire reason we are HERE is to turn our insides out, and fuck everything else around us.

So, I guess my question is -

When exactly do you think you might like to give it a go, this whole follow your flow and do what you were born to do, thing?

We've ESTABLISHED how rare it is to even KNOW, and you DO know, don't you?

What is it? The thing which you love so passionately, which takes you away, which when you step INTO it you just know -

This.

This is what I'm meant to be doing.

This is why flesh and bones become something.

This is the entire fucking reason I was BORN, and for the rest of my days I WILL DO THIS.

Say it. Say it aloud, your thing. SCREAM it aloud, right now, I dare you!

And then:

Become very sober and very still and VERY fucking honest and stare deep into the depths of the most SCAREDY-CAT part of your soul, and ask:

WHY THE FUCK AM I NOT DOING IT YET THEN?!

I can tell you -

From experience -

That if you don't do it?

It won't go away gorgeous.

It will NOT go away! What, you think that if you just keep pushing your truth down and getting on with the job of being whatever the fuck it is you imagine you need to be instead that your passion, your desire, your truth, will FADE?

Well -

Only if you die along the way.

Of course, you're as good as dead anyway, if you're not going to live anyway!

If you in any way don't agree with that right now, if you think I don't get it, or first this, or what about that, or it's not that simple, or that those other things that you give your life for instead MATTER, then okay-
Cool.

Thank you for showing yourself as not one of us.

It's fine.

I'm not here to speak to those who COULD have, who WOULD have, who just HAD to, first.

I'm here to speak to the ones who are crazy bold, daring, HONEST enough to know:

Nothing else matters.

Do what I came here to do.

Jump off the fucking CLIFF and just -

Just -

Live.

Let my heart beat.

Finally.

With the truth.

GIVE my life, fully.

For the truth.

LIVE my life, only -

For this.

For this.

For this.

There are few of us who ARE indeed crazy enough, bold enough, daring enough, or perhaps it's just that we MUST enough. I just don't have the patience ... I don't have it in me ... perhaps I'm too SELFISH ... to not live the life I was born for.

I tried.

It didn't take!

The desire didn't fade. In fact, it ate me alive. And the further I strayed?

The more everything just -

Became God forsaken fucking HORRIBLE.

I tried to eat, drink, escape, and busy my way out of knowing that what the real problem was, why I couldn't breathe at times, why I continually hurt myself each day, why I just couldn't seem to feel WORTHY enough ever, was all just a choice and it was a choice that I was making to live the wrong LIFE.

So, I walked away.

I RAN the fuck away.

I did it in a MOMENT, an INSTANT, a single tick of the clock and just because I knew that if I didn't leave it ALL behind I'd become ever more -
Trapped.

And I look at you -

And I wonder?

For how much longer? Will you allow yourself to live like that, be captured like that, stay TRAPPED like that?

For how much longer would you like, my dear, to continue to SUFFOCATE AND TORTURE YOUR OWN SOUL?

Maybe -

You're not really like me at all.

Maybe -

You just say you're an artist, and you're born for it, and you'll live for it and then die for it and you KNOW you ARE it.

Maybe -

You're actually like them.

Because really?

The thing which you love enough to live for, the thing which you'll live for until you'll die for, well, you can say it's your message, your truth, your art, and that you were BORN for it, but REALLY -

The evidence is simple.

The proof is all AROUND.
Your future is being written, now.

And it's here.

And it's here.

And it's everywhere you LOOK.

In your day.

In the way.

You give -

Of your time.

Your energy.

Your soul.

Your life.

Guess what?! This is the life you're choosing. No, it's NOT the one you talk of, dream of, wish for, and know in your heart you could HAVE.

It's this one.

Right now.

It's the one you LIVE for.

Your mission -

In life -
Should you choose to accept it -

Is to find the thing you can fall in love with and live for forever.

If you already found it and you're not now giving your ALL for it, then odds are?

You're actually one of THEM.

PROVE ME WRONG.

CHAPTER 7 - MAYBE YOU'RE JUST NOT A REAL ENTREPRENEUR

If you want to boil down every possible and available piece of advice about what it "really" takes to succeed, as well as everything you know inside of you to be ASBOLUTELY true, in the end, the only thing you ACTUALLY need to commit to doing is to stay the fucking course.

When the chips are down, and you feel like you're wrestling with fear demons while simultaneously sinking into quicksand - grit your teeth, and stay the fucking course.

When your offer isn't moving a single unit, despite you REALLY, REALLY knowing it's good and you REALLY, REALLY need the money, brush fear and freak-out off your shoulder like an annoying mosquito, and stay the fucking course.

When your mind is telling you to batten down the hatches! Sell everything! Start flinging scarcity offers out like a $2 hooker at a gypsy show to anyone who will pay it, slap yourself hard on each cheek, shake off the MADNESS, and stay the fucking course.

When you find yourself jumping up and down and 'look at me'ing' all over the internet, thinking that if you can just be the loudest! And shiniest! With the most bonuses! And extras! And discounts! And OMGGGGGGG!!!!!!!!'s! - take a BREATH, ask yourself if you actually feel good about how you're showing up right now, get connected back to your core and STAY THE FUCKING COURSE.

When day after day after day allows you to only JUST keep your head above water, you seem to be constantly counting pennies or having to rob Peter to pay Paul, you're SO damn sick of the struggle and the juggle and you just don't know if you can DO this anymore it's so damn TIRING and shouldn't you BE there already, stand up straight, square your shoulders, set your jaw, remind yourself who you damn ARE, and stay.the fucking.course.

No matter what is going on, working or not working, you're up, you're down, you're a motherfucking jack in the box with apparently 49 different emotional spectrums before

8am, either way the ONLY way you're ever going to get THROUGH it all and get to the Magical Land of THERE is by

Staying.

The.

Course.

And here is what to remind yourself of, when it's RELENTLESS and TUMULTUOUS and you just CAN'T EVEN, and you just want it to fucking WORK already -

Quite simply:

Shut the fuck up bitch.

This is the life you chose.

If it was EASY, everybody would do it.

Yeah, yeah, you were 'born for it' and you've always known you wouldn't live the normal life, you KNOW you are extraordinary and that your purpose work is POWERFUL. Well, guess what?

So do 16-gabillionty people who came before you and who are DEAD and who we never heard of, who never shone their light or got their true work out into the world.
Wanna know why?

They DID NOT STAY THE COURSE.

Many of 'em didn't even BEGIN. So yes, you get props for the fact that you're HERE, you're showing up, you've put yourself out there, you've LABELLED yourself an entrepreneur (hmmm ... truth is you either are or you're not INHERENTLY, it's not a label, but anyway ...) and you've invested time, money, effort, etc.

Good for you.

REALLY.

But also -

Meh. So the fuck what? Did it work yet? Is it working yet? Are you living your dream yet? No? Then it doesn't matter what you've laid on the line so far, or think you have. The truth is you'll only know JUST WHAT YOU HAD TO LAY ON THE LINE when you look back from a place of 'fuck me, I actually did it'.

The greater truth is most people will NEVER know, because they just won't stick with it to get to that point.

You think it's HARD, when you're dying and crying on the floor, when it's sucking every ounce of your energy, when fear is CHOKING you and your self-worth shit is looking you straight in the eye no matter which way you turn, when every bloody day you feel like you've gotta pick yourself up, bloodied and bruised, and go back out there swinging again?

Well, maybe it is hard. I DON'T KNOW. I don't know the depths to which you have to go, the turmoil and resistance you're being given to face. I know for SURE that only one in ten thousand people, if that, would put themselves through what I did to get to here.

This is not my ego talking ... this is me being very matter of fact about the level of fear and pain I withstood, and for how long. It's a FACT that the EXTREME vast majority of people would have caved.

Me, I stayed the fucking course.

And so now I get to play here.

It's REALLY that simple.

It was never a question of whether I would continue to take risks for my DREAMS ... it was ONLY ever a FACT that THIS IS THE LIFE I CHOSE, and so there literally was no other option.

Do what it takes.

No matter what it takes.

Until it takes.

Once you accept and CHOOSE that, and you actually freaking MEAN it, it's really quite EASY.

I mean -

It's motherfucking excruciating and you feel as though you go to hell and back every day; you are tested in ways you didn't even realise were possible -

But it's easy in the sense that you CUT OFF ALL OTHER OPTIONS.

Kinda like childbirth ... doesn't matter how horrific it is, once you committed to having that baby it was gonna come out one way or the other. You can say you changed your mind at various points (I definitely did that ... "I've decided to keep it in; I'm not gonna, y'know ... do that") ... but really, you know you have no choice.

You WILL fucking go through whatever you gotta go through.

And it will be worth it.

So, when I say it might be hard ... or it IS insanely hard to endure, right now, for you, well - sure.

But really -

Meh.

What does THAT have to do with anything?

It is what it is.

And so it is.

And it will pass.

But HOW hard, or painful, or terrifying it is, or how many times you fall on your face or feel as though your soul is being put through a mincer, well none of THAT has anything to do with whether you're gonna keep going, because you're IN IT NOW AND YOU HAVE NO CHOICE.

This is the life you chose.

This is the life you chose.
This is the life you chose.

And you WILL fucking take whatever it is you are GIVEN to learn and grow from, along the way.

If your mindset allows ANY sort of idea that there is SOME SORT OF OPTION TO CHOOSE DIFFERENTLY once in it, to back out - "no thanks, I've just, y'know, decided to NOT get the baby out" - then guess what:

YOU'RE NOT A REAL ENTREPRENEUR.

YOU NEVER WERE.

YOU NEVER WILL BE.

You're a normal playing dress ups with the idea of a freedom life.

Nothin' wrong with that ... everybody gets to have a little fantasy.

But when the dinner bell rings, time to go back to who you actually are, and that is NOT ONE OF US.

Too harsh?

Too bad.

This is how it is.

I don't say any of this to try and segregate, because you already ARE WHO YOU ARE anyway. I can't segregate or categorise ANYONE.

Your actions do that just fine and dandy for you already.

Your decisions.
The way you get back up or don't, when it's burning and tearing you limb from limb.

The KNOWLEDGE you already have, as to whether you WILL DO WHAT IT TAKES UNTIL IT TAKES AND TAKE WHATEVER YOU'RE DAMN GIVEN ALONG THE WAY, or whether there is even the smallest part of you which believes that at a certain point it would just be REASONABLE to back down, get a temporary job, whatever.

FUCK REASONABLE.

And fuck even the SMALLEST 'out'.

A REAL entrepreneur is not even CAPABLE of an out.

These are the facts.

If you don't like 'em, cool - a million people online will welcome you in with open arms and tell you 'there, there, it's okay, you can be half in and half out of COURSE you can, don't listen to the nasty lady"

We call these people the broke people who dream big and don't make shit happen.

By all means, if you're one of 'em and you can't deny it, go join 'em.

They are FILLED with platitudes and hustle bustle action which goes nowhere.

The COOL thing is, the lighter side of all I'm saying, is that it is SO fucking easy to get everything you want.

JUST DON'T QUIT.

Every damn day.

Get up.

Do what you gotta do.

No matter what.

Repeat.

COULD THERE EVEN BE AN EASIER FORMULA FOR SUCCESS?!

Stop fucking complicating it.

Stop looking for magic bullet answers instead of just being damn CONSISTENT.

And stop your bitching and moaning when shit ain't going the way you want it to. There'd only be anything to moan about if there were some sort of idea that doing 'x' should lead to 'y' and if it doesn't then you're going to huff off back to the normals.

If you're in it for life because it's who you ARE, then shit can get as infuriating as it likes and regardless, YOU will brush yourself off -

Pick yourself up -

Grit your teeth -

And stay the fucking course.

CHAPTER 8 - BE BOLD ENOUGH TO HOLD OUT FOR YOUR REAL DREAM

I told myself that maybe this was as good as it gets for me, maybe this is just how it is, maybe what I LONG for is just a fantasy, a dream, made up, NOT REAL LIFE, but the truth is I never believed that, you know?

I always thought -

When I looked inside -

When I looked to the FUTURE -

And when I listened to what was coming through me -

That actually, yeah -

I could kinda sorta have it all AND I would.

So, I held out.

I held out through the days in which money dwindled ever more, ever more, ever more.

I held out through the endless weeks and months in which it felt like every BREATH, every step, every MOMENT was painful, treacherous, and FILLED with risk.

And I held out, when my mind shrieked at me that I was crazy to imagine, to think, that it was possible, let alone for ME.

I held out.

I stayed the fucking course.

I just kept GOING, one day at a time, that's how it's DONE, and eventually?

Well -

Eventually.

Before we talk about eventually, let me ask you a question.

It's a BIG one ... and it requires a big and bold answer; a clear one, too.

DO YOU BELIEVE?

When you look inside, when you listen in, when you look to the future -

DO YOU BELIEVE -

That what you dream of -

Your TRUE dream, the fantasy one, where you have it ALL, and on your terms, no less -

IS going to become true?

Because let me tell you, if you can answer a hard yes to THAT, then THAT IS ALL YOU NEED.

You don't need to know how.

You don't need proof, not from ANYBODY else and not even your SELF.

You just need to KEEP PRESSING ON.

The hardest thing, I think, is not to do the work OF pressing on, really, but instead to keep the voices inside your head at bay.

Don't you find?

Just this past week I've noticed how RAMPANT they've been, when it comes to the relationship side of my life.

Telling me that maybe what I dream of isn't possible ...

Isn't available ...

Or maybe it's just not available for ME, maybe I don't get to HAVE it that good.

I dream of soulmate love ...

I dream of days filled with laughing and hysteria (the good kind!) ...

I dream of INCREDIBLE conversation that goes here and there and everywhere, and SO deep ...

I dream of astral travel sex and also some pretty next level on earth sex ...

I dream of deep connection -

Of KNOWING we are meant to be together -

Of looking into his eyes, and in there seeing my soul reflected back at me, and of the deep, deep certainty that this was the only way it was ever meant to be and ever COULD be.
And of all the fun and adventure and creation, which goes with it.

I imagine how it would BE, to be like that, and it feels, it feels, it feels ...

POSSIBLE.

Available.

And as though, surely, if I see it inside of me then it is MY DREAM TO DREAM AND AVAILABLE FOR ME, AND ALSO, NOW - ! that's just how it WORKS, I know this.

But then my mind chirps up -

My fear might rise -

Or perhaps I just get tired, and weary of waiting -

I find myself wondering - if it really has to be all THAT? If perhaps I'm holding out for too MUCH? If I'm just once again being this unrealistic crazy DIVA, and if I should settle -

Sacrifice -

Compromise -

Make do.

I find myself nearly almost sort of kind of BELIEVING this bullshit, and even beginning to lean INTO it!

And then -

At the final hour -

Or when my thoughts finally run their course -

A small still voice comes along, and whispers -

"But, didn't you dream such impossible dreams for your business Kat? Weren't you INSANELY unrealistic, demanding to the nth degree, you wanted it all, exactly how you wanted it, a business and life COMPLETELY on your terms, and you refused to give in?"

Well -

Yes.

That's true.

Your point?

Again, a whisper, or perhaps a tap on the shoulder this time -

"Well. Why don't you LOOK THE FUCK AROUND THEN GIRL?! At what you've created ... at what you allowed ... at who you ARE, and at all you now have ... get to do ... and be? Hmmm?!"

And with a toss of her head (she's a NEXT, next level diva, the voice inside my head!) she storms off.

Booty sashaying and hair all a-flying.

And I remember -

How I so VERY often nearly gave in.

How close I came to settling for making money doing what I kinda, sorta, almost NEARLY love ... if that's a thing!)

How many times I was SO scared, that if I held out for what I really wanted I would never GET there, and even if it WAS available, did I have the wherewithall to stay the course for THAT long, to keep going?!

I was so tired.

It was so never-ending.

And I felt so bloodied and bruised with it, a lot of the time.

But here is what I found to be true, without exception:

When I looked inside and was damn HONEST with myself, I found that in fact I ALWAYS DID BELIEVE.

In the end, I could simply never deny that I HAD FUCKING FAITH.

I knew I was born for it.

I knew I would make it.

I knew it was how it was destined to BE.

And secondly:

What I found to be true, without exception:

I could ALWAYS MAKE IT THROUGH THAT DAY.

I could always keep going for just one more day.

One foot forward.

PAINFUL as it was at times -

On the track I knew I had to BE on.

So often so scared -

Looking into the vast unknowing -

FULLY aware that I was laying myself on the line for something crazy, something exceptional, something largely unheard of!

But yes:

FULLY aware that what I felt inside of me was real.

Was available.

Was available for ME, or else I wouldn't be seeing and FEELING it.

And that ALL I had to do, ALL I had to do, was stay the fucking course.

So today if you feel you're fumbling ... falling ... maybe failing ... and you just don't know if you can keep going, maybe you should scale back your dreams, give in, just a little, REST, let 'reality' rule you ... which is to say fear ... then allow me to say THIS:

I'm with you baby.

I see you.

I am HERE with you.

When you're tired, dig DEEPER.

When you're weary, run FASTER.

When you feel your faith crumbling, grit your motherfucking teeth and decide to dream even BIGGER.

This is what we do.

This is who we are.

THIS IS THE LIFE WE CHOSE.

And God damn it, it's the one we're going to live.

It's VERY simple, in the end:

We do what others won't.

We get to live like they can't.

Just because they didn't tell you that the toughest part of this is holding out on the INNER stuff, doesn't make it any less true.

Do the damn work.

Have it all.

CHAPTER 9 - I KNOW YOU'RE A WANDERER, BORN TO BE FREE AND ROAM, AND I WANT TO TELL YOU, THIS -

I know you're a wanderer, born to be free and roam, and this is what I want to say to you.

It's okay.

It's okay that your soul is eternally restless and that as much as you try to settle it, stem it, find the thing, or the one, which will keep you, rest you, have you, hold you, allow you to be you, deep, deep, oh so deep down within where you mostly dare not look because oh! The tiredness of it at times! you know -

You'll never be done seeking.

It's okay.

It's okay that you want so desperately, at times, to be certain of the path ahead of you when the truth, which darling you and I BOTH know, is that you cannot see -

That which you cannot know -

And you cannot know -

That which has not been laid out -

And the path simply cannot BE -

Laid out -

Oh, so pretty and ready before you -
When, don't you see?

You are the one who must create it.

It's okay.

It's okay that this scares you.

That, in fact, perhaps this is the first time you really see this, feel this, know this, live this, breathe this, are this, the thing which really scares you?

Is to be you.

It's okay.

It's okay! That at times you don't know how to be you, you don't know what it means to be you, you don't know who can SHOW you how to be you, but if only you could SEE you.

It's okay.

It's okay that nobody told you -

That you didn't know -

That they didn't SHOW you -

That there is nothing to use as an EXAMPLE -

And yet you can still see SO FUCKING CLEARLY that the WHOLE freaking THING is about leaping -

And leaping -
And leaping -

And LEAPING -

Without a net, or, really -

Even the desire for one -

And that to leap.

Really!

Will be your destiny.

For always.

And always.

Amen.

It's okay.

It's okay that, at times, you're so RECKLESS, so STUPID, so FOOLISH, so foolhardy, and such a CHILD.

It's okay that you judge yourself more harshly than ANYBODY else could dare, would care, would know how, but that YOU still care -

That they like you.

That they want you.

That they need you.

That they VALIDATE you.

That they HOLD you.

It's okay!

It's okay that you want to say FUCK THE WORLD and SCREW THE RULES and I'LL DO WHAT I WANT and HELL TO THE YEAH but that when the going gets tough and your head hits the pillow and its night time and still and you feel SO fucking alone that all you want, at times, for a moment, and maybe it's not even TRUE, but still -

Is to feel accepted.

To be acknowledged.

And most of all?

To be seen.

It's okay.

It's okay that even though you can't see it, don't know it, can't FEEL it, that it's all just a MYSTERY that you DEFINITELY still know that part of it, most of all, fuck! Maybe all of it -

Is to be SEEN.

Be HEARD.

Be KNOWN.

And to lead.

Message.

Rule.

It's OKAY.

It's okay that you were born for so much MORE and that this DOES require you to be someone they COULD not, would not want, don't even THINK of, and that you ARE going to be judged for it, hated for it, cast AWAY for it.

It's OKAY. It's okay and you can MAKE it and you can DO this and you HAVE what it takes, and you can fucking OWN this and it's all -

Just -

O.FUCKING.KAY.

It's okay.

And it's okay.

And it's oKAY.

To be you.

All in.

All the WAY.

And FUCK THE WORLD!

It's okay and the sooner you SEE it's okay and LIVE it's okay
the better because here is what is SO not fucking okay.
It's NOT OKAY.

It's not okay. That you STILL don't fucking show up. That
you have this art inside of you. That you hold it in. That you
don't CARE. Because if you CARED about it you'd be LIVING
it and fuck YOU if you have anything to say aside from that.

It's NOT OKAY.

It's not okay. That after all this time. You don't fucking show
UP, and yes, I said it again and I'll say it again and I wish I
could SHOVE IT DOWN YOUR THROAT so you could actually
FEEL it.

It's NOT OKAY.

It's not OKAY. That you fight -

Not the world!

As you came here to do.

Not the FIGHT.

Which you were born to prevail in.

But instead!

That you fight your own God damn SELF.

What?

You think you still have TIME?

You think you have to get READY?
You think your fears are VALID?

IT'S.

NOT.

OKAY.

It's not okay that you BREAK your own spirit, day after day
after ever loving DAY, that you don't understand and live by
the truth OF the human spirit which is that we WANT to be

pushed we WANT to be confronted we ARE fucking gifted and we MUST let it OUT.

It's not OKAY.

It's not okay that you play -

Like a child -

A game of business and life like it's a freaking REHEARSAL and not even THAT because if you were truly rehearsing to PLAY LIFE you'd do it LIKE your life DEPENDED -

On it.

On you.

On this day.

On this moment.

On this NOW.

But instead?
You float.

And you maybe.

And you one day.

And you PRETEND.

That you're creating something.

Saying something.

Doing something.

Being something.

But what you're really showing?

Nothing.

We don't see you.

We don't know you.

We don't hear you.

And your greatest desire, in all of this, in the wandering and the seeking and the roaming and the never ENDING -

Was to be seen.

Be known.

Be heard.
For what's inside of you.

For what must come out of you.

For what you lock AWAY in you.

It's not okay.

That, as with all of those who you look to with scorn, or with sorrow, or with the imagining that THEY don't get it -

You're making a life.

As one of them.

You say you WILL, you say I AM, you say it's DONE, but don't you see?

If it was and it were?

We'd see it.

Show the fuck up.

CHAPTER 10 - MAKING MONEY ONLINE, LIVING LOCATION FREE, FINDING INNER HAPPINESS ONCE MORE AND GETTING BACK TO SHIT-HOT SHAPE: CAN YOU REALLY HAVE IT ALL?

Are you still wondering how you're going to make it work, whatever 'it' may be?

Living location free, having a successful online business, being your own boss, living a soul purpose driven life what EVER it is!

If that brain of yours is still DOUBTING, then you're going to love this chapter.

I wrote this a few years ago now about some incredibly inspiring clients I was working with at the time.

You need to realise that if it's possible for others then it IS possible for you.

These women DECIDED and took aligned action -

The question isn't IS it possible for you, or HOW are you going to make it happen -

The question is simply -

What are you going to CHOOSE?

Let's start with what Kim chose!

Kim joined my Society Inner Circle mentoring program and said hell yes to creating her dream business.

No website, no online business, no plan really at all, beyond what was mapped out at a two-day intensive weekend; a short retreat from her 9-5 'normal' life.

What she wanted? To be a freedom-based entrepreneur. And other things, but that's essentially the end of it.

Fast forward a few months later and things were damn freaking scary. A new business, the pressure of trying to actually make MONEY from it, of putting yourself out there? That's hard fucking work, never mind when you're still working full-time at a job that sucks the ever-living soul out of you.

THIS, of course, is where most people give in.

The majority:

I want it, I'll do what it takes, nothing will stop me!

And so they begin, excited and ready and CERTAIN that they can and they WILL.

Until:

Oh shit I have to actually WORK / keep going / pick myself up bloodied and bruised and broken and keep GOING?

I have to sacrifice abusing my BODY with stuff that blocks out the world and my ability to actually show UP in it?

I have to take a fucking real RISK?

Oh, no thanks.

That's okay.

I'll be just fine living like the rest of the fucking sheep.

Whilst getting fat, bored and borING

But hey, don't worry! I'm driven ... I have goals ... I just can't ACT on them yet, you know ... I'm busy ... stuff's going on ... you don't understand!

Anyway. Just a small side rant there!

But let's talk about Kim -

Right before Christmas, she came to me and said that something I'd mentioned on a training just HIT her:

Oh and if you're thinking this will be something mega profound, it's not. Except it is -

"If you don't DO it, you're not DOING it".

Isn't it funny how something so simple can suddenly make you realise you have to change EVERYTHING?

Like the realisation that life is NOW, or that you're not REALLY happy living like this, or that you could just START, or that if you're NOT doing it?

You're not doing it.

A day later, no joke, she quit her job. Just like that. Of course, she'd been WANTING to since we started together, and TALKING about getting to that point, but that was in July and this was Christmas; a couple days before if I remember correctly.

She literally came into the forum and made this announcement of realisation, and then ... acted on it.

Three weeks later she flew from Australia to Las Vegas to meet me for a two-day intensive, then went back home for three weeks or so, packed up her stuff, and met me in the Bahamas in February for our retreat.

She's traveling the world, location free, supported by a business that didn't exist ten months ago. Oh, and she still doesn't have a website :)

Which brings me to this:

Everything you know about business?

Is a lie.

You think there are RULES to follow, a process you must adhere to, and that you have to bide your time?

BULLSHIT.

A new entrepreneur friend of mine was telling me the other day how he went to 6-figures within mere MONTHS of starting out. 0 to 100, boom. He decided he was going to be THE #1 person in the world at what he does, and so he just ... did. With

NO online experience, I might add although he did, unshockingly enough, invest HEAVILY in working with the right mentors. He's on his way to 7-figures now and the best part?

Doing ONLY the fun stuff.

Now if you think that this stuff is a pipe dream for YOU, a few inspiring stories that get us all warm and fuzzy but far removed from the reality of what YOU can achieve?

Bull.

SHIT honey.

Of course, if that's what you want to believe ... that'll be your reality.

And I could tell you stories all DAY of real world women just like you, who started with nothing, no experience, and you can bet your ass JUST as scared and unsure of themselves but yet they did it because they refused NOT to, and yet you'd still have your list of reasons why you can't, not yet, not fully.

Of course, I'll go ahead and tell a few more stories anyway, since that's what I came here to do :)

And since the RIGHT people reading this? Will sit the fuck up and get to work; maybe this will be that so not profound, yet OH so profound moment of clickity-click clarity which we all need to be smacked in the face with from time to time.

If I can do that for one person with this chapter?

My work here is done.

So yes, you want to hear more? I got more.

Christine was another client of mine. She joined The Society on the same day as Kim, in fact! My inaugural two revolutionary leaders. These women and the others I lead at that level are like my heart, my core. My WHY, for sure. Christine came to me with an idea of who she wanted to be online, what she wanted to do, but it was clear that it was surface based. Vague. Not really the REAL stuff; the good stuff. She'll tell you that herself, don't worry - I'm not just smack talking here :)

But we got some clarity, and she got to work. HARD fucking work. The kind of work that requires laying yourself on the line, investing HEAVILY (in working with me, not to mention the actual time, effort, EVERYTHING) in order to build from scratch, a dream.

Dreams that aren't built on risk and giving it your ALL rarely come true. Or everyone would have 'em, wouldn't they?

Fast forward.

Five months I would say, it took, of relative PAIN. Good pain, for those who understand the concept. But pain. PRESSURE. You know what they say about diamonds and pressure? This woman went through the kind of internal transformation that most people wouldn't even want to READ about, let alone experience for a day or three.

And it took about five months, before the BIG shifts began. Sure, there were shifts along the way. And we worked CONSTANTLY. SHE worked ... I just did what I do, back into alignment, back into kicking ass.

This is one reason why I no longer take on short-term private coaching clients. Transformation doesn't happen in eight weeks baby! And whilst I'm all for doing deep dive work that lays the GROUNDWORK for transformation I no longer choose to do that at the higher level, with those I mentor personally.

Fast forward.

A few weeks ago, Christine left for Bali. Return: not quite known. She's location free.

Running her business.

Her ALIGNED business, not the one we first heard about in that room back in June last year.

She is one sick bitch :) ... and leading her own revolution of sick bitches committed to having a truly sick body, biz, AND life.

Hard work pays off.

But you have to be prepared to do the actual hard work, which is to say to fight - daily - the battle inside your own head.

You want more still? I could keep going all day!

Elles came along to my first London event. She lives in the Netherlands and is the kind of calm and reflective person who makes you suddenly aware of a whole lot of things you've been pushing away about yourself. Elles has this way of looking at you without really saying anything, where others would call bullshit (others like me :)) but she doesn't have to say anything at all.

Elles shared her BIG dream with us, in that room in London.

To have a farm, in Hawaii, where she could run spiritual retreats and the like.

We all laughed and talked about how we'd run my next retreat at Elles's farm in Hawaii.
You know when you laugh at something but it's not a joke? Well, Elles joined The Society that weekend, and every week since then we've done the work on alignment, on truth, on ACTING from truth. Her business has grown, from nothing, into something that is still growing (does it ever stop?!), becoming ever more personal, ever more REAL, her finish date at her day job now locked in for just a few months from now.

All good, if not great, right?

But something she wasn't telling me, even though we speak every week!

Elles came to my event in London last Friday, and the night before a group of my clients and I met for drinks.

"Something to tell you", she said.

"I wanted to wait until it was in person".

Oh yes, I thought - another big response on one of her guest posts, perhaps.

"We got the land."

"I've been asked to come and build it".

"We're moving to Hawaii in September."

Her husband, who is Tibetan, received his visa of residency in the Netherlands the same WEEK, which means he can actually move now.

Are you shitting me?

I couldn't believe it.
Except of course I believed it, I never saw it was one of 'those' dreams that people talk about.

And neither, I suppose, did she :)

You want something bad enough, you put your mind to it? You REFUSE to take no for an answer?

You fucking get it honey!

Rosemary. Rosemary, I think, is like my sister from another world, although I've never said that to her.

It's the high, HIGH level creator inside of her I connect with, the ARTIST within her she fought so hard to repress, trying instead to show the world what it wanted - what she thought it wanted - as a professional, as a 'business coach'.

I don't have to tell you ... if you're an ARTIST, a LEADER, a REVOLUTIONARY? Then honey you can NOT wear the title of business coach. Weight loss coach. ANY coach, really.

The truth is I don't even really work with coaches as my core clients, although many of my leaders DO coach.

But no, if you're a leader, a GAME CHANGER? You don't call yourself a coach.

But Rosemary, she was calling herself a coach. And she looked like a coach as well. A boring one, if we're being honest, or at least if we're comparing to who she actually IS!

What she wanted, was to show the world who she really is, but she wondered if she's too crazy for that.
"Yes", I said. "You definitely ARE crazy ... with your naturally damn crazy hair if you stop straightening it and let it fly, and your habit of breaking into song in the middle of coaching or sharing something ... there's no doubt about it, you are damn STRAIGHT crazy!"

Which is what you need to show the world.

And really why the fuck would you NOT want to be crazy; what's the alternative?

Fast forward.

The journey has been back and forth, as it always is. In the midst of lead generation, and client work, and selling, and all that has been the true work, which is the hardest work.

Making money is not actually the hardest work! Although sometimes you're tricked into thinking that. But for Rosemary the real work has been giving herself permission to SHOW the crazy. It's crept out in fits and starts, shoved back in at times and then let right out. Now it seems to be RIGHT out ... and the flow of ALL good things that flow has changed accordingly.

We went to dinner the other night, a special dinner with Rosemary and Elles and myself, my Society gals on the London side of the world, and over Italian tapas (!!) in Picadilly Circus, it really hit me:

Fuck me.

I've been seriously mis-judging these ladies, as well as the others who've stories I've told here, and others till who I haven't made mention of. This chapter is long enough!

I mean I talk to them every week ...
I KNOW what they're doing ...

I see when they get stuck ...

I help them move THROUGH ...

I give them feedback on their business and anything they want to bring up ...

And I've proudly watched them achieve their dreams, pretty much not at all in the way they thought they WOULD but get there - better than there! - nonetheless.

But here this whole time I just thought I was coaching.

And as I sat there on Friday night and really thought about what ALL these women have done in the past less-than-a-year, I realised:

This has NOTHING to do with growing an online business.

Sure ... businesses have been built.

But what's actually happened, really, is a revolution.

An individual one, for each of these women.

And a pretty damn powerful one from my point of view.

A year ago I set out to create a Society of REVOLUTIONARY leaders.

I was very specific in my head that I wanted to work exclusively with those who were called to MAKE millions, IMPACT millions, and to change the world. Which is to say, not about the numbers, but actual born leaders not 'women who want to make money online'.

There is a BIG difference.

And to be honest I kind of forgot about that dream. It's been a busy past twelve months what with life on the road, a new country every few weeks, the ups and downs of being location free as a family AND running and growing my own business!

And there's been times quite honestly when I've questioned what I'm doing.

Am I even helping anyone?

Is it even making a difference?

Does anyone actually NEED me?

Well the truth is I know that none of these women NEEDED me. They were freaking BORN with what it takes, and then they simply decided to act on it. Decided that if you're not DOING it ... you're not DOING it.

But I'll tell you this. And it's hard for me to say, because as much as I know I've helped people get a lot of results in business and in life, and it means a lot to me. But I guess my true calling - well I KNOW my true calling! - has always been to impact LEADERS, and those that want it all. To see them then rise up and GET it.

And there's been many times - even recently - when I've told myself I'm not there yet, I'm not leading in that way yet; how do I get there?

Until I sat down -

And talked to these women -

And really LOOKED at them, inside them, in a way we don't do in the flurry of our week to week conversations -

And was honestly just floored.

These women have actually changed who they were BEING. They've stepped into who they ARE. And they're LIVING that. And whilst THEY are the ones that did that, I can truly see where I in so many ways LED it.

I actually did it ... I'm actually doing it ... I'm leading leaders.

I'm starting a revolution ...

I'm seeing women all around the WORLD rise up and press play in a way that the 1% of the 1% doesn't even freaking consider.

It's pretty fucking awesome, if you wanna know. It's even more awesome that I know I'm just getting warmed up here!

And I guess that wasn't so hard to say after all :)

The majority:

I want it, I'll do what it takes, nothing will stop me!

And so they begin, excited, and ready, and CERTAIN that they can and they WILL.

Until:

Oh shit I have to actually WORK / keep going / pick myself up bloodied and bruised and broken and keep GOING?

I have to sacrifice abusing my BODY with stuff that blocks out the world and my ability to actually show UP in it?

I have to take a fucking real RISK?

Oh, no thanks.

That's okay.

I'll be just fine living like the rest of the fucking sheep.

Whilst getting fat, bored and borING

But hey, don't worry! I'm driven ... I have goals ... I just can't ACT on them yet, you know ... I'm busy ... stuff's going on ... you don't understand!

The majority watches life pass them by, one painstaking day at a time.

These women? They're not the majority honey.

And I suspect - strongly - that neither are you.

Go time beautiful.

Remember.

Life is Now. Press Play!

Kat x

EXTRACT FROM – STOP FUCKING AROUND AND FIGURE OUT WHAT YOU WANT FROM LIFE

Grab Your Copy On Amazon Now

Introduction

You were born with an inescapable need for more. 'More of what?' you ask. More of anything . . . more of everything!

From the moment you first tasted sugar, you wanted more of it.

The first time your grubby little hands found themselves unwrapping a new toy, your mind was being programmed for the idea of more.

When you grew old enough to understand trends, and your friends had cooler clothes, toys, or a better bike than you, your mind told you I want that! Then, you likely pestered your parents to get it for you.

As the years passed, you found yourself yearning for the right jeans, the perfect hairstyle, eventually the coolest car, and then the ultimate job.

Life is an eternal quest for more.

The bad news is you're never going to have everything you possibly COULD. If you stop and look around, it's always easy to spot someone whose life includes something yours doesn't.

The good news is there is an endless potential for more. No matter how deliberately you craft your life, there is always something else out there you can chase after. If you stop and look around, it's simple to spot new ideas for inspiration. It's easy to find proof that if you REALLY want it, you can have anything, do anything, and be anyone.

So the big question is, 'When are you going to stop fucking around and figure out what you really want from life?'

Chapter 1 - The Wasted Life

Schooling? Check. Basic or perhaps advanced skills in the essential 'must know' areas of life? Check. Tertiary education? Check. A job? Of course! A mortgage, a partner, and a couple of kids? If you don't already have them, they're probably on the way.

For many people, being able to say 'Yes, I did it!' to these desires means they've reached the pinnacle of success. They've DONE it. They've met the world's standards, and because they never stopped to consider if their own standards matched, they're happy and content. Eventually, however, they're not.

This can happen slowly, insidiously, like a festering wound that begins sometime in the mid-to-late twenties, or it can come on suddenly at any time and completely without warning as if a slap in the face.

Shit. Is this what my life boils down to?

When did it happen for you?

Stop fucking around. Do this instead.

Start thinking about how life could be if you actually consciously created it. Oh - and keep reading. :)

For more kickass books for kickass women, including free downloads go to:
www.booksforkickasswomen.com

SO WHAT NOW?

As a thank-you for reading my book I'd like to invite you to join my FREE Video Training on Choosing Faith Over Fear to Create the Business and Life You're Meant For!

You can jump in right now and begin this incredible training right now!

https://thekatrinaruthshow.com/faithvsfearfreetraining

"Choosing Faith Over Fear to Create the Business and Life You're Meant For!"

Connecting back to higher self and soul, in order to build your biz & life by following the blueprint you were **BORN** with!

What I share in this short video training will, without a bit of exaggeration, **bring you to complete stillness and CERTAINTY** about how you know you're meant to be showing up right now.

When I first started out in online business, I had no clue I was even about to be in online business *(I was just writing a blog)*, firstly, but secondly, there were **no rules of online marketing.**

I was one of the early adopters ... and that was a good thing, it means **I followed intuitive, purpose, passion, flow, and that voice inside my head!**

As time went on, and more and more 'experts' popped up, I decided to learn **how to do it even better** than what I'd already figured out by myself. High achiever much? Of course!!

Well, what happened, really, was a HUGE exercise in remembering to **JUST BE ME**. Over about an 18 month period I slowly softly nearly killed my own soul trying to do it right and be 'proper'.

Eventually? **I gave in to that voice inside.** The one that said I knew better than ANYBODY about what is right for me. Even if, maybe especially if, it meant flying blind / shooting from the hip / making shit up as I go / all of the above!!

Since then, since deciding to be led by **FAITH** not **FEAR**, in all areas of my life, I have created a multi 7-figure purpose led empire, and more importantly?

A from soul and truly **FUCK YES** life!

Today let's talk about how to do just that for you. *You KNOW the answers are within.*

So,

If you're ready to say yes to YOU –

To being fully and UNAPOLOGETICALLY you –

And going ALL IN, at BEING you -

And choose FAITH not FEAR -

Then I'd like to share this gift with you.

"Choosing Faith Over Fear to Create the Business and Life You're Meant For!"

Connecting back to higher self and soul, in order to build your biz & life by following the blueprint you were **BORN** with!

Yes?

YES.

Join me here, now -

https://thekatrinaruthshow.com/faithvsfearfreetraining

Community and Client Love

'I'm so grateful for the guidance you shared with me - you pulled out a deep fear and pain that I have been holding onto for 1.5 years and it had got to the point where I didn't even really notice it anymore.. it was almost normal... and in one swift sentence you rocked my world and cracked me open in the best way.

Which led me to journaling on the most gorgeous beach in Bali so connected to my higher self and my higher mission. Thank you so much for serving in this way.'

Alecia Repp

'WOW is all I can say. My soul DEMANDED that I participate. The biggest breakthrough I've had has been liberation from my doubt. I now KNOW that my soul desires will not be denied when I simply stay in gratitude and faith. That the only way for me to thrive is to be in perfect alignment with my truth, my values, my message.

Fuck the rules. Fuck everyone else's judgement of what my success must look like. It's all about me. It's all about me creating my art and the rest just follows. Like magic. The result - I am grounded AF. I believe in myself. I trust myself. I share my message from my heart and I ONLY take the aligned action.

I have completely transformed the way in which I do business and I'm loving it! I have freed myself in my personal and business relationships. Quite frankly the journey has only just begun. THIS is the path and I will not waiver again. So much love and gratitude to Kat and every woman who shared the journey with me.

Anel Bester

'The moment I was ENERGETICALLY drawn into the vortex that is Kat I knew I had found what my heart was missing... permission.

Permission to do what I want, not what I thought I had to do.
Permission to recode.
Permission to upgrade.

I've worked with Kat in several programs including one on one and each time I'm guided to the exact answers I need to continue growing, not just as a business owner but as a person as well.

I can't recommend her enough, from her shenanigans, general disregard for the rules, and willingness to be the messenger, she has truly been and continues to be an amazing mentor."

LaTisha D Styles

"Kat is a life changer for sure!

Before Kat I was terrified to be my full self, I thought I had to be the polished off version (as I had been taught by others) and now since following Kat and working with her I have been being my fully expressed self which is so healing in itself!

I have magnetized so much good into my life that would not have come by being that other version of me.

Kat will take you to your true soul self.
She is a guide from beyond and super intuitive.
She will see your Soul and bring it out.
She will unfuck your brain around every subject.

Take her courses, buy everything she is selling, absorb her wisdom, your life will change in ways you never thought possible (but deep down always knew).

I know she is a soul sister of mine and so grateful for her. I'm so excited for all she will do next.

Love you Kat!!!"

Britney Taylor

'Kat, I just cannot thank you enough for helping to bring outta me what I've always had - and never knew it.

For 33 years I've been in my own fitness gig. But, only in the past 11 months that I've known you I've become a certified personal trainer, built a private clientele, opened my very own studio, holding group classes, training youth athletes. And already have my eye on the open space in the building next to my studio.

I swear it's all the big and little things you said and did that actually made me think, 'why the hell not? Let's do this!'

And for that, I am eternally grateful to you. I have no idea how much further I'll grow in my business, but I'm open to every possibility, because of you.'

Karah Schwalm

"THIS WORKS!

YESSSS!! Just created, launched and sold the first spot to my very first online group training program for book writing success....

All in the space of 2 hours!! BOOM!!"

Dave Thompson

"Loving the content and your fire and love Katrina Ruth.

It's a real fresh kick up the butt with lots of soul love and soul business which I'm loving. Thank you!

Already got my money's worth not that, that is a big deal but wow love the value and just straight up clarity, purpose and direction here.

I'm showing up with bigger dreams and aspirations and feeling the transmission of this work booting my soul in direction. Again thanks Kat love your work."

Rhyn Nasser

"Oh My God!!!! And Oh My God!!! Again!

I'm still in so big shock! After 5 very hard days just started to go through your course Kat and... I'm so shocked and excited and I just can't believe that I'm here!!! There are so much information, so many things which help to bring business to life! I'm really, really completely shocked as I worked with many coaches but no one have given as much as you have Katrina!

Thank you!"

Sylwia Pupekr

"I have literally being going from OMFG highs to being in tears just listening to you and working through the exercises you give.

When you are live-streaming to us it feels like I'm in the company of the greatest friend there ever could be, and also the most admirable people I've had the honour to connect with.

I feel so truly honoured that you've made yourself available in the ways you have, and I am sitting here with tears streaming down my face, because it feels like there is a knowing and being seen."

Joelene Rose Michaela Jane Longbow

_____

"THE AMAZING IMPACT THAT KATRINA RUTH HAS HAD ON MY LIFE

In 2016, I came across this HOT, bossy, fit chic online called Kat Loterzo who I instantly adored! I giggled at her truths that triggered many (back then she was much bossier) and her content totally HOOKED me!

I was a frumpy online entrepreneur at the time who wasn't getting very far. I was low in confidence and stuck in a lonely marriage that I knew no way out of.

Fast forward to now.

Thanks to Katrina Ruth, I have become fit, healthy, vibrant, independent and so much more of ME. I live in a beautiful apartment overlooking lake Geneva and my kids live between me and their dad. It all worked out well.

I had a photoshoot today and I had a few different outfits with me. The photographer teamed a pink top I had been wearing with shorts, with a black leather skirt I have. She then gave me the slightly too big blue heels I'm wearing in the photo below - I don't normally wear heels, I can't walk in them.

Afterwards she sent me a few untouched photos (she will make them shiny) but this one really made me gasp. It's not intentional, but it's very much like Kat used to dress... and I look pretty fit in it. Not that I'm intending or wanting to look like a Kat clone, but it did make me think about how far I have come and I wanted to share that here.

Because if you right now are feeling frumpy, stuck, scared and low in confidence... you have the power to change your situation.

With determination, discipline, commitment, a massive dose of self-belief and a brilliant mentor, you will transform your life.

It's never too late by the way. I'm 8 years older than Kat and I'M ONLY JUST GETTING STARTED!!

Thank you Katrina Ruth. I adore you!

To our success, happiness, joy and abundance!"

Niamh Maria

_____

ABOUT THE AUTHOR, KATRINA RUTH (FORMERLY KAT LOTERZO)

Katrina Ruth (previously Kat Loterzo) is an entrepreneur and writer based on Australia's sunny Gold Coast. When she isn't furiously unleashing her true message via her daily blog 'The Daily Asskickery', or her #PurposeChurchwithKat live videos, she is running her multi-million dollar online coaching business as an entertainer, speaker and success mentor to 'the crazy ones'.

With 50+ self-published books (mostly Amazon best sellers), over a decade in online business, and several hundred soul-led product and program launches under her belt, Katrina is known as a 'Content Queen' who just doesn't stop. She believes that you CAN have it all, on your terms, so long as you're willing to get honest with yourself about what you're really here to do in the world, and her great mission in life is to help you find who you are - and then become it.

Before transitioning into her current work Katrina initially built a 7-figure online fitness business by following zero of the 'rules' around internet marketing, and to this day her process includes the truth that YOU know best what is right for you and your audience. Now, as a mentor, she kicks the butts of the worlds top entrepreneurs, leaders, visionaries and creators and is arguably the most hardcore chick online.

Katrina lives with her 2 children in her dream home overlooking the ocean. She is obsessed with great coffee, great wifi, great wine and great training of the mind and body, as well as creating as much content as humanly possible on the topic of alignment and taking MASSIVE fucking action.

Katrina is also an expert in "No B.S" coaching and would love to help you create a business and life you love, completely on your terms!

Learn more about Katrina at:

www.thekatrinaruthshow.com/about/

Follow Kat here:

Facebook: www.facebook.com/lifeisnow.pressplay
Instagram:
www.instagram.com/thekatrinaruthshow
YouTube: www.youtube.com/c/thekatrinaruthshow
Ebooks: https://www.booksforkickasswomen.com

Sign up for Kat's FREE Video Training on 'Choosing Faith Over Fear to Create the Business and Life You're Meant For' By choosing Faith over Fear I've now created a multi 7-figure purpose led empire, from soul. A **HELL YES** life!

https://thekatrinaruthshow.com/faithvsfearfreetraining

MORE BOOKS FOR KICKASS ENTREPRENEURS

For more kickass books for kickass women (& men):
www.booksforkickasswomen.com

Also, don't forget to follow me on Facebook, to keep in touch and get access to my latest Blog posts.

It would be my absolute honour and pleasure to have you in my community and give you the motivation, inspiration, education and butt-kickin' empowerment you need to get out there and create the business and life of your dreams!

I have to warn you though ... my style is somewhat out there. I'm not gonna hold back on saying what I think. I may very well call you on your sh*t ... often. And if I think you're limiting your ability to create what you WANT to create and CAN create then I'll be coming down on you like a ton of bricks. Loving bricks, but still.

YOUR HELP PLEASE!

Did you enjoy this book, find it helpful, or love how it kicked your ass?

I'd love it if you could take 2 minutes of your time to leave a review for this book on Amazon, even if you purchased it direct from my website and not from Amazon. Just search for this book and my name on your Amazon site.

Thank you so much!

And don't forget –

Life is Now. Press Play!

Kat x